THE PERSISTENCE
OF MEMORY

THE PERSISTENCE OF MEMORY

POEMS BY

MARY FELL

RANDOM HOUSE
NEW YORK

Portions of this work have previously appeared in the
following publications: *Columbia, Little Apple, Panache,
Quindaro, Tendril, West End Magazine*, and
Worcester Review.

"The Triangle Fire" originally appeared as a limited-
edition, hand-sewn chapbook published by Shadow Press,
USA.

Library of Congress Cataloging in Publication Data
Fell, Mary.
The persistence of memory.
I. Title.
PS3556.E472P4   1984   811'.54   83–43189
ISBN 0–394–72363–5 (pbk.)

Manufactured in the United States of America
Typography and binding design by J. K. Lambert
98765432

For my parents, Paul and Betty Fell

*The National Poetry Series was established in 1978
to publish five collections of poetry annually through
five participating publishers. The manuscripts are
selected by five poets of national reputation. Publica-
tion is funded by James A. Michener, Edward J.
Piszek, The Ford Foundation, The Witter Bynner
Foundation, and the five publishers—Doubleday,
E. P. Dutton, Harper & Row, Random House, and
Holt, Rinehart & Winston.*

THE NATIONAL POETRY SERIES, 1984

Wendy Battin, *In the Solar Wind* (Selected by
    William Matthews)
Ronald Johnson, *Ark 50* (Selected by Charles Simic)
James Galvin, *God's Mistress* (Selected by
    Marvin Bell)
Mary Fell, *The Persistence of Memory* (Selected by
    Madeline DeFrees)
Stephen Dobyns, *Black Dog, Red Dog* (Selected by
    Robert Haas)

Because everything burns repeatedly
or keeps burning

—CHRIS GILBERT

CONTENTS

ONE

THE TRIANGLE FIRE

1. Havdallah

This is the great divide
by which God split
the world:
on the Sabbath side
he granted rest,
eternal toiling
on the workday side.

But even one
revolution of the world
is an empty promise
where bosses
where bills to pay
respect no heavenly bargains.
Until each day is ours

let us pour
darkness in a dish
and set it on fire,
bless those who labor
as we pray, praise God
his holy name,
strike for the rest.

2. Among the Dead

First a lace of smoke
decorated the air of the workroom,
the far wall unfolded
into fire. The elevator shaft
spun out flames like a bobbin,
the last car sank.
I leaped for the cable,
my only chance. Woven steel
burned my hands as I wound
to the bottom.

I opened my eyes. I was lying
in the street. Water and blood
washed the cobbles, the sky
rained ash. A pair of shoes
lay beside me, in them
two blistered feet.
I saw the weave in the fabric
of a girl's good coat,
the wilted nosegay pinned to her collar.
Not flowers, what I breathed then,
awake among the dead.

3. *Asch Building*

In a window,
lovers embrace
haloed by light.
He kisses her, holds her
gently, lets her go
nine stories to the street.

Even the small ones
put on weight
as they fall:
eleven thousand pounds split
the fireman's net,
implode the deadlights

on the Greene Street side,
until the basement catches them
and holds. Here
two faceless ones are found
folded neatly over the steam pipes
like dropped rags.

I like the one
on that smoky ledge, taking stock
in the sky's deliberate mirror.
She gives her hat
to wind, noting its style,
spills her week's pay

from its envelope, a joke
on those who pretend
heaven provides, and chooses
where there is no choice
to marry air, to make
a disposition of her life.

4. Personal Effects

One lady's
handbag, containing
rosary beads, elevated
railroad ticket, small pin
with picture, pocket knife,
one small purse containing
$1.68 in cash,
handkerchiefs,
a small mirror, a pair of gloves,
two thimbles, a Spanish
comb, one yellow metal ring,
five keys, one
fancy glove button,
one lady's handbag containing
one gent's watch case
number of movement 6418593
and a $1 bill,
one half dozen postal cards,
a buttonhook, a man's photo,
a man's garter,
a razor strap,
one portion of limb and hair
of human being.

5. Industrialist's Dream

This one's
dependable won't
fall apart
under pressure doesn't
lie down on the job
doesn't leave early
come late
won't join unions
strike
ask for a raise
unlike one hundred
forty six
others I could name
who couldn't
take the heat this one's
still at her machine
and doubtless
of spotless moral
character you
can tell by the bones
pure white
this one

does what she's told
and you don't hear
her complaining.

6. *The Witness*

Woman, I might have watched you
sashay down Washington Street
some warm spring evening
when work let out,
your one thin dress
finally right for the weather,
an ankle pretty
as any flower's stem, full
breasts the moon's envy, eyes bold
or modest as you passed me by.

I might have thought, as heat
climbed from the pavement,
what soft work you'd make
for a man like me:
even the time clock, thief of hours,
kinder, and the long day
passing in a dream.
Cradled in that dream
I might have slept
forever, but today's nightmare

vision woke me:
your arms aflame, wings
of fire, and you a falling star,
a terrible lump of coal
in the burning street.
No dream, your hair of smoke,
your blackened face.
No dream the fist I make,
taking your hand
of ashes in my own.

7. *Cortege*

A cold rain comforts the sky.
Everything ash-colored under clouds.
I take my place in the crowd,

move without will as the procession moves,
a gray wave breaking against the street.
Up ahead, one hundred and forty seven

coffins float, wreckage of lives. I follow
the box without a name. In it
whose hand encloses whose heart? Whose mouth

presses the air toward a scream?
She is no one, the one I claim
as sister. When the familiar is tagged

and taken away, she remains.
I do not mourn her. I mourn no one.
I do not praise her. No one

is left to praise. Seventy years after
her death, I walk in March rain behind her.
She travels before me into the dark.

TWO

ACCOUNTING

In my thirty-fourth year, the weather
shakes out leaves, rheumatic trees

ache in early frost. Armatrading sings
far off, where bodies I love

turn in distant sleep.
I tally losses,

two hands' worth, one
the friend who fell this year,

lovelier than leaf,
who swallows earth at thirty-six.

I am content in this new place
alone. I suffer the usual

complaints: too much bourbon
to ease my smoky throat, familiar heat

for the doe-eyed impossible student.
People are kind. I doubt

myself. I write home *don't forget me*
and they don't.

OUT-OF-LUCK, MASSACHUSETTS

The town that couldn't be licked
gives up, sunk
between these hills. The sacred
heart beats fainter, blessing the poor
in spirit. Boarded-up
factories litter the river. It does no good,
town fathers knitting their brows,
there's not enough shoe leather left
to buy a meal. In company houses
the unemployed wear out
their welcome. Diminished
roads run east, west, anywhere
better than here.

DRIVING OUT OF SOUTHERN WORCESTER COUNTY

say goodbye to small towns
their boundaries cutting across the names
of dead indians, trees
still remembering that speech

their shelved histories leaning on
years of drought, of rain, lives
the immigrant knows nothing of

canadian, pole, latin
root their lives on rock
this earth won't give up

their names the journey a word took
changed but familiar, unaware of footsteps
echoing years back in the forest

their lives held like a cup, thin and intricate
that could break with a sound like water falling
or the sound of an animal running for shelter

but strong with an old craft
hard, and made to be passed on

to their children

or to tourists who look out from car windows

bored, and unknowingly carry them off

THIS IS A LOVE POEM

My blood
suddenly
knows you are gone

It is shouting your name

It runs
down to the ends of my fingers
looking for you

It wants to be
a piece of red wool
unraveling
all the way to Central America

It wants to be a boat
coming into the harbor at Managua
carrying fruit

Through all the rooms of my body
it is running
opening doors

A child in a tantrum stamps
red shoes
demanding to know where you are

ROADBLOCK

I stop the car. A sun,
huge, orange, blocks the road.
River on fire. Blackened trees

float in it like kindling.
In the highest branches, a rainbow
trout swims graceful arcs.

A dove mourns in deep water.
Now trees lower
the sun to the river. I could

breathe water now, fish
this sky for comfort.
But something in me tears

the world apart, puts fish
in the river, birds in trees, and the sun,
a boundary marker, between.

I turn, get back in the car and drive
across the bridge. Dark is building
a town on the opposite shore.

THE TETHER

The car nudges the hill
where Dead Horse climbs. This engine
isn't balky like the last one
you kept alive so long.

                 Quiet now.
You like to pretend you don't know
where this road leads. I lean back,
watch the headlights nuzzle trees,
the narrow road too stingy
in the dark. Welcome the woods
that take us in.

              You ask
do I want to. I slide your body
from its envelope of clothes.
Smell of dust, ripe fruit, salt.
Where night leaves off, I start
to run, your hand the tether
letting me go, bringing me back.

BASIC TRAINING

In the kitchen my mother is cooking.
We are watching World War Two
in the living room. A voice says
Pearl Harbor has just been attacked.
My mother's cry, a broken plate.

When the alarm rings, we march
into the school basement where it's safer.
If there isn't time,
crouch under a desk for protection
from atom bombs.

We practice jungle belly crawl
through the high grass in Gordon's yard,
Red Ryder air rifles cradled in our elbows.
For sneaking up on enemies, walk
heel first, then the whole foot, quietly.

Take a bottle cap. Gouge out
the cork heart. Put it inside your shirt
over your own heart, the cap outside.
Push them back together:
a war medal.

Heroes limp from battle
at Park Theater, an eye out
for enemies in the dark aisles.
Near the candy stand, a secret nod to the clerk.
She knows who we are.

On every street corner, granite markers
named for soldiers.
They have come home
to squat forever, like the rest of us,
on the curbstones.

AMERICAN LEGION

To all veterans
of all wars
of the Main South area

After work he straggles in, tired of fighting.
He shoulders through the line of men,
lays his arms on the bar and orders a tall one.

But there's this pain near his heart
where something went in he can't wash out.
He and the others bathe their wounds

with stories each agrees to swallow.
As they drink down the long afternoon
his morale rises. So he slams down the phone

when the wife calls to ask if her old man's
ever coming home for supper
getting cold on the kitchen table.

No matter that later she'll dish it up
on plates that explode against the ceiling.
For now her husband sits at the bar

where he ties one on like a decoration
and bends his elbow in slow salute
to himself and his fellow soldiers.

NOT WORKING

"a man of your experience" they say
offering nothing
and him laboring forty years

as though to have bread on the table
were enough
he should sit up and beg for that
the bastards

and them so smug, smiling
holding out their soft hands
as if they knew what hands were for

he knows:
not for nothing he's worked
these calluses into his palms, the flesh
hard and ungentle

it's not work he needs
but his own name spoken here
and thoughts that go down
easy and soundless
as the beer in this glass

ENTREPRENEUR

It's no crime to take things,
like life, a little at a time.
At Brown Shoe Company he stitches
leather on the big machines, careful
not to sink the needle into his own hide.

There is no choice but work,
no luck but money:
a good boot, strong sole
brings ten dollars on the street.
At lunchtime, on five-minute breaks

he lets them fly
out of windows, land by the factory wall
where he finds them later
walking home.
He names greed the thief:

someone else's stealing seventeen cases
puts guards at stockroom doors,
alarms on walls, throws
his modest business
off for weeks.

THE PRACTICE

We lived on Winter Street. Bricks escaped from factory walls, distraught. Ours was a building with too many corners. Families got lost and were never heard from again, small names gathering dust or pinned to the wallpaper like religious medals, their blue ribbons fading.

Every step shook plaster from the ceilings. We carried it into the street on our shoulders. Whole rooms blew away by morning. Old aunts went on shopping trips and never returned. Dishes vanished as we ate breakfast. My own mother disappeared one day into her bedclothes, thinking she was better off.

All my life it's been like this. I tell you, there's no sense believing what you see. I learned early to practice not being fooled.

CROSSING

I was dreaming of church bells,
their ponderous flight on Sunday air,
throaty birds let go from the white
limb of the steeple:

only the tin cups and plates
clucking against the wagon, as the wheels climb
out of another chuckhole on the prairie.

What would they say, those women
in feathered hats flocked 'round the preacher,
their men strutting in Sabbath best,
if they saw how eagerly
this soul takes wing from the tight laces
of bodice and home that bound it in?

Here, grace is simply
getting rid of the unnecessary:
the fine piano with its ivory keys
powerless to unlock the wagon wheels from mud,
the lace curtains helpless
against dust and sun.
Pared down to usefulness,
I have not time or need for the tame

luxury of sin, nor breath except to pray
our holy cache of water will hold out
to the next spring, the dwindling flour
stretch to dress our tired bones.

This Sunday morning, blessed
to be alive as I pass the trailside crosses,
the oxen's moaned organ notes accompany me.
Strength to go on is the only sacred thing.

A PEASANT LIFE

A woman holds by the sleeve a bundle of rags, five years old, neither male nor female, merely round, made of various garments and woolen scarves. This is the old country way of protecting children from illness, cold, from the bad eye of evildoers, by disgusing them as something else. So I was dressed up, by my own family, as a pitchfork—legs rigid, arms close at my sides—until one day I was stolen from the barn. My mother chased the thief, cursing him loudly, and striking him with a broom—my sister. Too late she realized her mistake, hearing our cries, and took us home to soothe us by the fire. We forgave her, of course, knowing she meant no harm. From then on we decided to pose as ourselves, inviting, in this manner, only those troubles which truly belong to our lives.

THREE

FISHWIFE

At night you throw
nets to the river.
I work on the bank

in lantern light,
the blade of my knife
catching fire.

The bellies of fish
glisten, small moons.
I gouge them red, scrape off

the starry scales.
Sometimes I get sad
studying the drowned

constellations of eggs.
Husband, it's late,
we will be old soon.

I lift my dress.
Out there on the water
can you see my breasts

reflecting, moon white?
Old fish,
I have baited my hook.

Come here where I wait
to catch you
in this red creel.

HUNGER

When you come home
there's supper waiting,
beans, cornbread
nothing else.
You could cut
the bitterness between us,
plenty of that to go around.

I never thought it would
come to this, you
had a way with a girl,
I liked your body
against me, print
of your mouth on my breast.
Never thought about

two hungry kids, each fall
two pair of shoes to buy,
how there's no stopping
children growing even when
crops won't grow at all.
Don't look at me that way,
I know you do your best.

Think I like sleeping
alone, only a bare wall
to warm my back?
You say I'm cold, I'm
just getting older,
asking who pays
for every taste you get.

THE COOK

1. the potato

From among blind stones
they dug out this
many-eyed beauty,
jewel of the island.
Thick-skinned, like them,
with a soft white center,
its value more than gems:
bread and meat it was,
a heart
shaped like their own,
that kept on beating
until it blackened
and returned them to the ground.

2. *the cow*

A cow is good luck,
if you've got one—otherwise
you dream your days
of shaking hands with one.
Just be polite,
introduce yourself, and with your own
gently pry those benevolent fingers loose
. . . King Midas couldn't touch
into purer gold
what pours from her moneybag!
Magic it is, too,
how she can change into riches
the grass of any poor field:
not like the unlucky Irish
who tried it
and died with the blades still green
in their discontented mouths.

3. *the mistress*

Madam
has little to complain about
and no need to fret over waste
as others do. Six good
years of my life I've filled
her delicate belly, and never once
scorched the soup.
And if I take it as my due,
her brags to well-fed friends
that I'm a treasure,
it's no excess of pride:
as lumps of coal are pressed
into diamonds
by the unbearable weight of the world
so in deep mines
of hunger was I formed
and there's no one has
a better way with food
as one who's starved.

4. the recipe

Steam rattles the pot lids
on the stove, a roiling odor
of earth escaping doomed vegetables,
the tang of raw meat bloodies the air,
from the oven, warm fingers
of bread are reaching . . .
and though I eat each moment whole,
though my flesh ripens
like a fruit tree with its burden, still
something goes hungry in me:
a girl needs more than meat on her bones,
more than milk, so deeply to dream
the world away, the coarse
body of things to which she must waken—
and waking too soon,
the dream untasted, craves all her days
in whatever she eats,
salt or sweet,
that exact, irretrievable flavor.

MOONSHEE

He cries, he cries
too much. His ears
redden like poppies.

The neck a stem
that can't hold up his head,
wet blossom.

I hold him on the crescent
of my hip, stalk off
across the muddy fields

to bring him to Miss Annie.
She peers into his eyes, opens
the tight buds of his fists.

She says he's got
a withering disease, I must
do this, and this.

He makes it through the spring,
she says, he'll live,
though he'll be puny.

She ties a poultice bag
around his wrist.
Going home, I do

for luck,
the thing she taught me,
and lift him to the sky

to watch the moon,
the night's first tooth,
come up.

SHEEP'S CLOTHING

Hung tail down from a fence post,
warning to chicken thieves, fatal signal
against poaching in violent farmyards,
your thick fur, garroted
throat say *coyote*

but I know, wolf, some trickster's
got you believing in him
instead of yourself, charmed you
so you can't hear the clean
heart-biting note that knows you,
fooled you into thinking
you belong in that dog-eared chorus.

But when night comes, dropping
stars like bones, you'll sharpen
your teeth on them, stare into dark until
your vision clears, listen to growling
wind in the trees and escape,
howling:

the marks on your throat swear
you've done it before.

UNION ROAD

The air is green today,
as if the drowsing land could wish
color into these winter drabs.
But the way that pine asserts itself,
and wheeling birds call down
a certain intensity of light . . .
In a month, perhaps, the willows
by the road will cloud.
Though snow lies still
between the corn rows, I feel
spring's slow idea begin
to grow in me.

ONLY CONNECT

Here crows attend their raucous school.
Today's lesson: how fence and fields are one
question to be solved by a feather's length
floated between them. How each thing
is connected to every other thing. To learn
that knotting of the wing which ties together
sky, fence, barn, field, wire,
that leap into air that pulls the air behind it
like a string. And the trees? The trees
are nothing, until they throw their nets
against the world, and drag it in.

HOW BLUE IS IT?

It's all been said about the sky before
so why bother? It's useless
to remark its color this late
February afternoon, the exact moment
that the winter pall has lifted.
And if it seems kinder, somehow,
the way it strokes the flanks
of grazing cows, or visits
the solitary fences, don't make mention.
Let's get back to work, and not waste
time asking, how blue is it?

Because she can see for miles
in any direction, she is not afraid
of the unexpected. If the road bucks
under the tamarack, the next hill
is so much the same she thinks
she hasn't moved. White houses,
white land, white sky. Horses,
a smudge of cows. Red barn
where fields surrender
flags of corn. Her life, the white line
on the highway. She's followed it
this far. The future appears
predictable. Distance the car she drives.

DRIVING IN FOG

If I were lost in one of these fields
among the anonymous corn
I wouldn't know which way to turn
home, or toward some nameless town
with its church and peeling feed store.
The tail of a horse is patient; it sweeps
a window in the fog, while the hooves of a horse
run away across the stubble.
I think this must be what it is like
when the last breath goes, and we wake
in the new dimension. I may be a ghost
like the others, dressed in my tattered clothes,
the crows bits of black cloth
the wind blows past me. And if in the past
I could say, I'm not afraid of anything,
now I am afraid, deeply afraid,
of nothing, and how like smoke the air is
here where it burns.

NEBRASKA

Out on the plains, trees
are dying of loneliness.
Immigrants came, seeds blown
thousands of miles, to put down here
their baggage of roots and branches.
How the heart longs for its old companions!
The tongue searches the mouth
for familiar sound.

A farmer shows me dishes
his ancestors carried to an empty place.
He is building a house to hold them.
Animals die in his traps, or escape
chewing off their delicate forelegs.
Here a tree has torn itself up by the roots
and tried to run away.

I am leaving these farms behind me
in sleep. Expanding sky dissolves
the flat roads. In night fields
crows fly home.

MIDWEST LULLABY

The moon is rocking
in its cradle of wheat.
There's a star hung from the sky
to amuse that fat white baby.
Coyote's tired, he forgets
to cry, and the corn grows quiet
wrapped in its husk of sleep.

FOUR

UNHOLY DEVOTIONS

All my girlhood
the ringing of
bells measured out:

this one
to kneel for, this
to get up, this one

complaining *my fault*
and beating its breast.
I got sick

of the sour looks, those saints
grumbling in their bathrobes.
Whose fault I turned

to another faith, that old
hand-in-his-pants
the priest never heard of?

He works
in mysterious ways
the Good Book said.

And sure it's a miracle
the way that it
takes them, men

strayed from the church
these twenty years shouting
God's name with such devotion.

So *let it be done
unto me,* I prayed.
And they did.

CHINATOWN, 1873

On the night avenue
I am a brag
in my red dress: *I dare you.*
My small feet, pointed breasts.
The look in men's eyes.
Coin blossoms in their palms.
Under their touch
I am stone, I refuse
to bloom.

For this I was stolen
from sleep, a girl
sold away from all flowers.
My mother cried, my father
counted money.

The sky dark.
In my sleep the stars
gutter down.
Lotus flowers
on a pond, wax petals.
My face
floats on the water
where it has fallen.

THE PROPHECY

The old neighborhood remains. Some call it Green Island, remembering the canal that cut through it, now underground. Built by Irish laborers, the canal gave Water Street its name. Jews still run their shops there, though they've moved their families to the other side of town. No one goes down in the basements anymore. Rats the size of dogs, they say. Kids in the Catholic school learn Polish prayers. And on Millbury and Harding Streets, everyone talks big stories in the same old bars.

At Kelly Square, the streets come together to form a star. Immigrants followed it here, Poles, Irish and Jews settling along its five arms. Green Street was my father's point on the star. His mother, Aggie, made whiskey in her own still. Though she and her husband were American born, Patsy spoke all his life with a slight brogue. Winter nights, the cop on the beat would come in from the cold to warm himself with Aggie's brew. Putting his little glass under the still, where whiskey squeezed into it drop by drop, he'd run out to the callbox to tell the station all was well. When he got back the glass would be full.

She made beer, too, and it was the children's job to get rid of the discarded malts and hops. Though she warned them not to, they threw them in the sewers which, come spring, would froth and bubble.

As if it were funny, my father tells how neighborhood kids went out to search the tracks for coal, each lump a treasure. His old friend Milly laughs and says how she held up her skirt when a train went past, tempting the railroad men to throw her coal.

Though my father is a storyteller, he has little else to say. When he was ten his mother died. He can't remember his grandparents or their names. A few photographs survive, some unidentified.

JOAN: THE APPROACH

I was born to do this

When all is at last ready
according to the way it was revealed:
sword, armor, charger, your flag of lilies
on a white field; when the sun rises
and foot soldiers and the doubting
men-at-arms assemble at the gate,
and the townspeople, hungry for miracles,
have cheered you on, and the priest
has blessed and absolved you;
when everything is prepared you ride out
into the rising heat, although
in the end nothing will save you:
not saints nor God nor angels; accused
as a whore and a witch, you will confess,
finally, that you are the angel,
that even your voices betrayed you;
but when all is ready, and the day burning
that you were born for, you ride out
because nothing will save you
if you stay.

THE RAGMAN'S LAST REEL

It was a kind of fame
not enough and
not quite what he had dreamt of
years ago
but on better days
the wagon was a stagecoach
and he booted and spurred
and the old horse's flanks turned silver
on the long ride

Then in a way
he could say he was a hero
saving folks from parts
they had outgrown

It was at night
the script got bad
he was an outlaw
alone in the hills
and nobody
looking for him

So when the good roles
started running out
he set his barn on fire
and went inside

It was so bright

like riding into the sunset

NICK

the old man
the no-legged man
named

nick

sits on the stump
of his body
waving his make-believe
legs

with these
elephant legs
these
trunks of trees
he tells stories of how
the war was won

he knows what it is
never to touch
ground again

in a place
of cut-off things
he floats

like a gold watch
like a pendulum

in dreams he's
lighter than air

he flies
like a bullet through the night sky

he swings

like the medal
pinned to a general's chest

THE VETERAN'S WIFE

show me no maps
no histories

I want to forget
that day's look
the way the sunlight broke
apart his boy's face
and never
set it right again

oh I was a parade and he
a flag waving goodbye
from the steps of the last train

I have what the war sent back
a look I cannot answer
I try to sing him to sleep
I don't know
what he wants from me

I put away my dishes and my plates
all there is
he is a weight
I carry through these rooms

no photographs remark
what becomes of things

IN COAL

The sun gets up and lords it
over the stooped hills. Below him
Brood and Blue, those bent old women,
shake out their sooty aprons at the town.

Going out, my husband lifts
his arm against the light
that hurts his eyes.
Last night he saw timbers falling
in his sleep, his hands
digging air as if it was dirt.

I've sunk all I've got in that mine.
All day I feel its mouth at my neck
like some rich old landlord
I owe back rent.
I'll spend this morning sweeping
dust out of the shack.
It's the one thing I can count on
sure to come back.

Tonight when sky turns anthracite
and one star burns, a miner's lamp,
I'll take my wish to the gate
and wait for him
to rise one more time. He'll have
two dollars in his pocket,
a coal-black face. He'll be wearing
the moon in his mouth.

PICKET LINE IN AUTUMN

This face getting brown
as morning falls
just ripe out of the sky—
a change from last night's
cold, warm gloves and
frost poured into
these empty coffee cups—

you've never been so much
in the world as now,
spending all daylight
and all night too outdoors,
going in circles like the world does,
though sometimes it seems
standing still, getting nowhere—

except you know your tired feet
are turning the earth
and someday the sun
will give itself up to you,
the leaves surrender—
you know they will, if
you keep on walking long enough.

KEEPING VIGIL

Sparrows blow like cinders
out of burnt air. Main Street
smokes under sodium lamps.
Sirens fly south.

Cars break down, worn out
by the weight of sky.
They rust all night where the moon
on Canterbury Street
cries over junkyards.

Near Union Station, groan
of boxcars coupling,
the catcall of a passing train.
Drunks hug their doorways,
made lonely by the sound.

In our house, my mother
puts out the lights.
The ballgame is turned off

in my father's dream.
On the back porch clothesline
a few stars are hung out.

I am one wish
left burning.

THE PERSISTENCE OF MEMORY

Phillip Dufault's stolen
cigarette, cribbed from the inside left
pocket of his father's suitcoat
and carried in Phillip's own
jacket, with the blood-red legend
Woodland Prep, over the cage
of his clamoring heart, up
the cobbled hill, into the secret
air of the barn,

ascends through a hundred years'
stink of horses, past hay
the color of horse piss,
to the dusty loft; is blessed,
broken, shared among worshipful boys
attendant at this mystery,
come to consider,
in the sweet smoke curling the rafters,
meaning, and not give a damn,
and who, because of what was only
the step of the wind on the guilty stairs,
stub it out and hastily descend
into fugitive daylight,
leaving behind the cigarette which

has already forgotten them
and even now

smokes above the asthmatic
breath of the galled horse stamping
its hoof in the wooden stall,
over the ancient wagons, around
cracked bridles and old bits
sprouting grass in their hinges,

smolders, a length of fuse
that wanders the afternoon, dawdles
through evening, curls into the sleep
of the children next door,
igniting bad dreams,
calls out the neighbors to look,
wakes sirens on Main Street,
throws water on nearby rooftops,
scorches the trunks of trees,
turns weeds to black lace,
lights candles
of grass in the yard,
empties the lot, and
reduces the barn to ash.

MARY FELL was born in 1947 in Worcester, Massa-
chusetts. After several years as a social worker, she
enrolled in the MFA Program at the University of
Massachusetts, receiving her degree in 1981. She
now lives in Richmond, Indiana, where she teaches
English at Indiana University's East Campus.